Dedication

To those who wonder, to those who hope

all the care in the world

Logistics

Hi, if you like this project, please send me back some pictures with your face and some of your favorite poems legibly in them. Algorithms on Instagram like faces, so to spread the project, I will use the image to promote the process. You could also just post a pic of yourself with the book to your Facebook story and tag me @kitcmartin. More than anything, it's about activating networks, so if you have any other cool ways to share, happy to join in the mischief.

Tip Jar

Additionally, if the work moves you, please tip accordingly. Venmo me $5 @kitmartin or PayPal me kitcmartin@gmail.com

Zen of Corona

Zen of Corona

Kit Martin

1 HERO PAY, CHEAP HAZARD PAY

You pay me to feed your kids
You want it on the shelf
Assured attendance?
But it ain't enough
Before all this you never held my hand
Took it for granted, I could pay my rent.

One question? When will it end?
$3 an hour to stock your beer
I am grateful you're paying for my danger
But also, you care that I am here?

Strike these strangers
Who won't cover their face
Hero pay you say,
Then you spit in my place
My man's out of work I cover our kids
They won't get hungry as long as I don't get sick

One question? When will it end?
$3 an hour to stock your beer
I am grateful you're paying for my danger
But also, you care that I am here?

Give me protection Not $2 even
We are dying in thousands
For your booboo tastes.
I can't help feeling hero pay doesn't pay
You know my kids are alone at home today

One question? When will it end?
$3 an hour to stock your beer
I am grateful you're paying for my danger
But also, you care that I am here?

2 OPEN

Enough is enough. It's not up here

I am not minimizing Covid, because it's real
It just not up here
How are we gonna lend a hand, if we can't stand?
We gotta make a Living.

We know in New York it's exploded,
And we really do care,
It's just not up here
It's not up here.

Pay-check to pay-check families, are at the food
bank
How much can we take?
Farmers are pouring food on the ground,
Waste abounds,
And it's not up here, it's not up here.

Small business could take the risk,
But they draw a crowd.
We can't gather now,
If you're not smart, and do it right
You get infected through town.

The government is trying,
And people are dying,
It doesn't feel it's around,
And it's not up here,
So what do I have to fear?

28 dead at the nursing home,
Dying alone
I remember thinking,
Maybe we will be spared
But it won't be so fair.

You combine the sickness with the cries of poverty,
You get "I asked my 2500 Facebook friends if they
had it. To a T, no one did."

3 YESTERYEAR

I took the road out of Chicago, just south.
It winds by the lake and comes on an unknown
shore.
By the lake, like a sea, our things gather in
eddies in the tide.
Those ideas left there with the rocks and sand.
Drift wood grows.

Flipping through the corridors, by where we
used to talk about Tamagotchi, we sit.
We find in the discarded something we can
use.
Moss and wood, sand and bones.

At the far tip of land we see the end of the
world.
There we uproot our tree.
There by the tree the edge of that world was
findable and clear.

We knew that.
Did they though?

4 THE ZEN OF CORONA

With new cases at or approaching zero, have confidence to open up — albeit it cautiously.

Alcohol spray and tiny disposable bags for storing masks are at every table.

I fear death. If they don't take my temperature, I won't go inside.

I think we all fear it could be any of us.

The worker herself risks infection everywhere.

Second wave they say. So frightening.
I will smile,
Take each day.
I will do my job, because I get people where they are going.
I am proud of my job.

5 DYING WHERE YOU LIVE

As the virus sweeps the world it's stopped up
the search for Muslim burial plots that face
toward Mecca.

While bodies pile up, for lack of a well
oriented grave, more Muslims turn to French
cemetery soil to bury their dead.

Under normal circumstances, we fly the
bodies thousands of miles. Now we pile them
here.

Fear of infection makes it impossible to
repatriate the corpse to lie next to his brothers
and sisters' bodies.

Two dozen wooden grave markers pegged
into the ground demonstrate the recent deluge
of death on the graveyard.

Willing to be buried where you lived is one
kind of integration.

6 SITTING IN THAT MONEY

Small businesses sit on the money granted to pay their fired workers, unsure how to spend it.

What is the point of hiring workers without toil to give them. Come back ye unyielding soil, so our workers' yoke can be broke.

They want to stack up the money as cushion to soften their future falls. I wish I had a pillow too, I think.

All you fat cats, start a delivery service, drop off diapers to those in need. Could make you rich.

How can we be sure we are following the rules

The rules are still being written... and with so many typewriters furloughed he added.

The loans will be forgiven,
if workers keep getting paid,
if the money is spent in eight weeks,
if the rules don't change.

Owners would prefer to hold onto the money
until the toil hours are longer
But the S.B.A. won't say.
She didn't have any debt.
Taking on some, as we go down the shitter
scares her.

I felt it was predatory, she said.
Coyote Ugly got itself a loan
All it's people let go
It thought it could stay on

On April 22nd Lovell furloughed Ugley's
hangers on. She said she didn't have much of
a choice. She didn't see the point in paying
'em around with every one gone.

And so the money meant for me and you
hangs out in the Ugliest account unused.

Our understanding is, it's to pay the workers.
But when that money runs out, what are we to
do? Fire them again?

Ventilation is like the exhaust pipe of the
body.

After two weeks of care, we are having
trouble ventilating her.

7 VACCINE

At 1:00 am on March 21, 1963,
A little girl named Jeryl had come down with
the mumps,
It just so happened her daddy was a designer,
of medical vaccines,
So he rushed up to work, and came back to
her in a breeze.
Staying up all night, in his broken down lab,
Turned his swab of her throat into the best
chance she ever had.
Weakening that virus, until it became a cure,
stopping the mumps from all it could incur.

8 RENT STRIKE

Halt rent
We can't pay
Open up money grubbing another day.

#canelrent
Protest in cars to keep distant

AOC supports
up ending housing payments

"To cancel rent would require
For the Constitution to expire"

Ilhan Omar introduced
The Rent and Cancellation Act

Which would cancel rent
And foment landlord discontent.

9 THE BURDEN FALLS ON WOMEN

I Believe a woman,
The burden has been placed on women to defend him.

If this is true, it could take down #metoo,
Powerful women staking their name,
On what a groper has claimed.

Without more truth, it's all claims,
who to believe and who to contain.

In the end, it's the American people who have to decide.

So where do ya stand on Biden's hands?

10 NETWORKED

Metcalfe noted the value of a network rises in proportion to the square of the number of users:

$$n(n-1)/2.$$

This enables agglomeration. **Value** increases in proportion to the square of your contacts.

It also enables pandemic. **Harm** goes up in proportion to the square of your contacts.

Farr's law, it's the curve we have flattened.

Open is better than closed. Your notions obey Metcalfe's, not Farr's law.
Ideas network too.

C3.ai made a Covid data lake.
We can all explore it.

Social distancing has slowed the spread. Fewer people died. But how many unborn ideas died between them?

The value of both connection and insulation rise in proportion to the square of your contacts.

11 IBM

"believe that when people and technology work together, we can create a world that's more open.

More collaborative and productive. More adaptable to change. More resilient than ever before."

12 REVOLUTIONARY

Eliot management funds Eko's suit over a revolutionary idea.

In video streams play different videos depending on how the person orients their phone.

Progress really is incremental.

13 THE FUTURE

So what happens when the capitalist machine turns back on?

I think we can all now better imagine what climate action would look like: the clear skies as our octane addiction has taken a hiatus allows the sun to shine.

I feel we can better see what open streets would be like. Kids and cars and bikes all roaming together like a village square.

I think more people may come to feel what isolation is like, and better empathize with those capitalism marginalizes.

I don't think of it as a machine, we will turn back on. Instead it's a fabric, and this has changed the very fibers that hold it together. Each change is small, but I think we'll feel the difference.

14 THE DEVIL GETS MADE

I wonder if the devil gets made
When someone Jackhammers
Someone takes my wife
Someone leaves their bets undone

I wonder if the devil gets made
When they drop their beer
Steal my cheer
Break my back

I wonder if the devil gets made tonight!

15 ELECTION 2020

In a big bright land, with 328 million people
Working
Finding love
And toilet paper

Just six states decide our fates,
it's
Arizona, North Carolina, Michigan, Florida
Pennsylvania, and Wisconsin, who'll settle our
hand.

16 FREE

This little voice in my head has started to whisper:

"Buy a car, buy a car. You can be free."

17 CRITICAL VACUUM

99% of releases never get reviewed.

Most academic articles are read only by their author.

Most dating profiles get zero likes.

What makes us worthy to critique?

18 FREE GAS

What to do when gas is free?
Constrain supply to you and me.
We should not have energy,
unless we pay profitability.
"Growth is a disease that plagues the space," we need to cure to interest pique.
To rob us blind of wages meek, companies keep us from freedom deep.

Should we have free energy?
But built by what? For who to keep?

19 THE WORLD BENEATH MY FEET

Cataglyphis running her fast legs across the hot Wadi Rum desert sands. She is notable for the fact she navigates using the spectralization of the sky. As light passes through the atmosphere, the differing thickness of the air changes what wavelengths get through. So these dears can see the purple near the horizon and the yellow directly overhead. They navigate so across the hot open desert sands. A real pleasure to spend a day with them.

20 PEOPLE MOVED

Seattle officials clear Ballard encampment, raising concerns about where homeless can go during coronavirus pandemic

This headline is so misleading, it should read:

People with jobs, wearing uniforms, forced people without jobs, not wearing uniforms to move. The people that were forced wondered where they were supposed to go once evicted from their home.

21 I'M WATCHING YOU

The pandemic's consequences are far
reaching.
It's going to change the ways we work.
It's no longer gonna be 'is it fun?'

Now it's gonna be.
is it safe?
is it resilient?

At first:
stickers on the floor
extra cleaning
desks spaced apart.

Then, staggered shifts.

Now, a social distancing app.
points for every time you keep 6 feet
I can see my own score. The company can see
all our scores.

Now, three levels:
the young previously sick,
the under 65 without hypertension,
the old smokers

The company complains, medical data is
protected.

Now watching:
measuring proximity
Bluetooth and Wi-Fi makes a tracing app
answer a questionnaire, get to work
take a selfie. If you're not too hot, get to work

Turnstiles, and X Rays at offices once were
deemed intrusive
Now they are ubiquitous.

22 COMMUNITY

Add to the list of what we know now,
wilderness is not as far as we seemed.

The birds go cheep
The coyotes go wooh
The deer go tumbling by.
The boars a-go a-barreling
Right under our noses all the time.

To see a coyote on my street, in broad daylight,
nonetheless
Gets me to like these tourists better than the
usual ones, I confess

So get out there and watch them, those wild
wonderous creatures

They're living right at your door, so no protest features

Getting spotted day by day, as humans stay inside:

The birds go cheep
The coyotes go wooh
The deer go tumbling by.
The boars a-go a-barreling
Right under our noses all the time.

We live in a world full of animals
We just have to observe them

Get a little closer to our four-legged city dwellers.

Go on!
howl like a coyote,
Cheep like a bird
And please go tumbling by.
Always a-go a-barreling
Like the boar at night

To embrace our furry friends
You never know where it will take you
In this big big world of kin.

23 STRATEGIC RESERVE

A Nebraska City $ees no Choice but to keep
working
We keep things on shelves, in barrels, and in
fields in mass
Call it national security,
But we don't keep the processes that make
them
That's you 'n me.

We need to not only lock away commodities,
We need to also lock away the ability to create
them

Make a strategic reserve of face mask makers,
iPhone placers
Or Sewing wherewithal
It will help us keep the practice going whatever
the journey will entail

24 FACTORIES

3D printed elbow extenders,
so workers can avoid door handles

We now leave 15 minutes early, so no
overlapping shifts
Of course that makes it hard to tell the next,
what I've been doing

So I give them a call, or shoot them a text
to keep the chain a-going.

The company now makes its own Viru Clean,
and gives it away to all,

These are all tricks we learned from China
in no time at all.

25 HIJACKS

Her lungs inflamed. Tiny air sacks drowning.
Kidneys failing in shock from the assault.

When recovering, his left leg swailed.
A blood clot in his deep vein.

Covid is nothing to play with. It's in our hearts,
minds, stomach, lungs, kidneys and veins.

26 YOU DON'T HAVE TO...

While inside, be productive, so the saying goes:
Carve a wood
Write a play
Ingest philosophy

Gain a sense of a mastery
Restore self-control.

Plant a garden
Flourishing and green

But the thoughts of failure hold us back

"I am going to fail", "Perfection is the aim" and
feeling overwhelmed.

Take those feelings learned through lifelong
trauma,
And break them down into nicely wrapped
little presents for yourself to unwrap.

And remind yourself, unwrapping presents is good for you. Valium helps.

Only keep friends who cajole you to keep being productive.

You can do whatever you want if you put your mind to it.

Including, play video games and watch Sling TV.

27 RICH SON, POOR SON

4:15 minutes a day,
Jacob learns through play.
Counting out the carrots
for his project today.

Just across the way,
another young man stays.
Waiting for his lunch,
he didn't see his teacher till May.

The costs of education,
an unequal provocation.
To those who have
we give zoom.
To those without
we give doom.

Spotty Wi-Fi
breaks the learning.
Uneducated masses
still churning

To one day
be free.

Free of want
Free to love
Free to their ownself be true

But in this land
born to free,
our education system ubherds.

28 I MISS

I miss the going,
I miss isolation in a crowd

I miss people's faces
I mask my sadness

I confess, I miss the bar
I miss the sunrise through the
coffeeshop window

I miss variety
I long for what's been taken.
Hope for her return.

Nostalgia for the commute, the office, the park
by church.

31 WAGE

Wages for housework are only fair.

32 UNTITLED DESTINATION

For the thousands of kids who ran the border
The immigration fight grinds on.

Through webcam, from shelters they plead.
Stop the cases during a crisis!

Think school is complicated remotely?
Think of national expulsion over zoom.

Some say the calls resolve minor obstruction
Clear the roll for later deportation

Others argue, children should participate in
their case. That we should not rush in the face
of decimation.

The judge sits in facemask, in a mostly empty
room,

Judges the twelve to seventeen years old's.

33 BREATH

Notice how no one says just breathe during a respiratory illness?

34 THE OFFICE

Small box.
Protects me from offshore
Impromptu chats.

No small box.
Jobs go where they are cheapest
No more office rent, floor cleaning dent.

"I mean, if you'd said three months ago
that 90% of our employees will be working
from home
and the firm would be functioning fine,
I'd say that is a test I'm not prepared to take
 because the downside of being wrong on that
is massive,"
said Morgan Stanley Chief Executive James
Gorman in mid-April on the bank's earnings
call.

While many can work from home,
People who create benefit from being around others
And people who collaborate find it easier in the same place.
Young people need to network
Stock traders for instance rely on high speed infrastructure
Folks with small children or apartments prefer to work from an office

Not to mention physical space is good to safeguard data and watch employees

Engineering is the only part of a snowmobile making company that is losing working from home. Notably, that is the only creative part.

35 WHY DO PICTURES MAKE SENSE?

Picasso said, The world doesn't make sense, why should my pictures?

Mostly because stories make sense.

Stories contain Beginning, Middle, and End.

Pictures are part of narrative, not the world.

36 👽ATION

I feel so desperately the need to work with people on my creative pursuits

but also, the complete 👽ation CoViD and late age capitalism cause.

37 **RUSH, NO RUSH**

If I don't paint nails, the money fails
In a pandemic work is anemic

Tricia demands a manicure
In a national glampocalypse

We tiptoed and ran towards the freedom of
open, like black Friday shoppers who got
stampeded by late stage capitalist pre-
vocational demands.

We all want a calling,
right now
that call demands resumption of consumption.

38 PROTEST

You rested your knee on my head.

I can't breathe

My eyes closed, reported dead

George Floyd, 46

In result, we rose up and said the system is wrong,

Wrong to sit, wrong to rest,
wrong to generate ages of anguish.

I can't breathe.

Black lives matter, including my own.

FIN

Made in United States
North Haven, CT
30 November 2022

27540955R00038